Counting the Stars at Night

Counting the Stars at Night

The Complete Works in Verse and Prose

Yoon Dong-ju

With Three Poems Translated by
Insoo Lee

Translated and Introduced by
Sung-Il Lee

RESOURCE *Publications* · Eugene, Oregon

COUNTING THE STARS AT NIGHT
The Complete Works in Verse and Prose

Copyright © 2022, Sung-Il Lee. All rights reserved. Except for brief quotations in critical publications or reviews, no part of this book may be reproduced in any manner without prior written permission from the publisher. Write: Permissions, Wipf and Stock Publishers, 199 W. 8th Ave., Suite 3, Eugene, OR 97401.

Resource Publications
An Imprint of Wipf and Stock Publishers
199 W. 8th Ave., Suite 3
Eugene, OR 97401

www.wipfandstock.com

PAPERBACK ISBN: 978-1-6667-3883-4
HARDCOVER ISBN: 978-1-6667-3884-1
EBOOK ISBN: 978-1-6667-3885-8

To the Memory of
Yoon Dong-ju (1917–1945),
Whose soul must have become
A star in the sky at night

죽는 날까지 하늘을 우르러
한 점 부끄럼이 없기를,
잎새에 이는 바람에도
나는 괴로워했다.
별을 노래하는 마음으로
모든 죽어가는 것을 사랑해야지
그리고 나안테 주어진 길을
거러가야씨것다.

오늘밤에도 별이 바람에 스치운다.

1941. 11. 20.

Holograph Manuscript of "Prologue"
(Yoon Dong-ju Memorial Library, Yonsei University)

Contents

Introduction   13

Poetry

Prologue   27
Self-Portrait   28
A Boy   29
A Snowy Map   30
Returning at Night   31
At a Hospital   32
A New Road   33
A Street without Signboards   34
Primeval Morn (1)   35
Primeval Morn (2) (Translated by Insoo Lee)   36
Till Dawn Breaks   37
A Terrible Hour   38
The Cross   39
Wind Blows   40
A Sad People   41
Walk with Your Eyes Closed   42
Another Home (Translated by Insoo Lee)   43
The Road   44
Counting the Stars at Night (Translated by Insoo Lee)   45
White Shadows   47
A Beloved Memory   48
A Flowing Street   49
A Poem Written Easily   50
Spring (1)   51
A Confession   52
Liver   53
Sleepless Nights   54
Consolation   55
Eightfold Blessing   56
Mountain Water   57
An Ailing Rose   58

Like the Moon 59
The Pepper Patch 60
Cosmos 61
A Portrait of My Younger Brother 62
A Wonder 63
The Temple of Love 64
A Rainy Night 65
A Dying Man's Wish 66
Window 67
An Afternoon in a Glen 68
Piro Peak 69
The Sea 70
Pensive Moment 71
Pathos 72
Downpour 73
That Woman 74
Thermometer 75
Landscape 76
Moonlit Night 77
Market 78
Night 79
Twilight Turns into a Sea 80
Morning 81
An Autumn Night 82
Washed Clothes Hung over a String 83
A Road in the Valley 84
Chickens (1) 85
Forest 86
The Sunlit Side 87
Mountain Top 88
Chest (1) 89
Chest (2) 90
Twilight 91
Southern Sky 92
Dream Has Shattered 93
On Such a Day 94

Soccer Field in the Afternoon   95
Lark   96
Upon Moran Peak   97
Meal Ticket   98
Bidding Farewell   99
Pigeons   100
Firmament   101
Daydreaming   102
On the Street   103
There's No Such a Thing as Tomorrow   104
Life and Death   105
That Single Candle   106
Echo   107
The Cricket and I   108
Dawn Comes with the Baby's Crying   109
Sunflower's Face   110
Sunlight and Wind   111
Trees   112
Mandol   113
Grandpa   114
Firefly Light   115
Both   116
What a Lie!   117
Pockets   118
Winter   119
Chickens (2)   120
Snow (1)   121
Apple   122
Snow (2)   123
Pattern for Footwear   124
A Letter   125
A Dog   126
Sparrows   127
Spring (2)   128
What Do They Eat to Live?   129
Chimney   130

Airplane   131
Rain in Sunshine   132
Broomstick   133
An Old Couple of Roof Tiles   134
Map on a Sleeping Pad   135
Chicks   136
My Old Home   137
Clam Shell   138
The Hill of Turgenev   139

Prose

Shooting at the Moon   143
Where a Shooting Star Fell   145
Flowers Bloom in the Garden   147
The End and the Beginning   150

Index of Titles   155

About the Translators   159

Introduction

The Life of Yoon Dong-ju

Yoon Dong-ju was born in 1917 in a small town in Manchuria, where his parents, as many Koreans did in those days, lived in self-exile, so to speak, away from their homeland. His initiation into poetry started early in his boyhood: when he was only twelve, he was already engrossed in writing songs to be printed in what he and his classmates claimed to be their 'literary journal.' Upon graduating from a high school in Manchuria in 1938, he entered Chosŏn Christian College (later, Yŏnhi Liberal Arts College), in Seoul, built and run by American missionaries, and graduated from it in 1941. To celebrate his graduation from that college he had a collection of his poems published in a slim volume, entitled *Sky, Wind, Stars, and Poesy* ('하늘과 바람과 별과 시'). After graduating from the college, upon his father's urge he went to Japan for further studies, and entered Rikkyo University's English Department in 1942; but for some unknown reason, he transferred to Doshisha University's English Department in the same year.

In the summer of 1943, when he was getting ready for a brief trip to home, he was arrested by the Japanese police on the charge of getting involved in a political activity, and soon put in Fukuoka Prison. In those days, Koreans considered to be intellectuals were under police surveillance. The only reason for the arrest and imprisonment of Yoon Dong-ju was that he happened to be a cousin of Song Mong-kyu, who was also studying in Japan at that time. A student attending Kyoto University, Song Mong-kyu apparently was then participating in clandestine activities for the cause of having national sovereignty restored. When a few relatives and friends visited Yoon Dong-ju at the prison, he told them that everyday he had to receive injection of some unidentified 'medicine.' On February 16, 1945, he died in prison. According to a jailor of the prison, right before dying at dawn-break, Yoon Dong-ju gave out a loud scream, which he could not understand. Was it a word uttered in protestation to God, or in acceptance of his fate to have his body and soul ravished by political butchers? When Yoon Dong-ju breathed his last breath, it was in a prison cell in a country where he went to study English literature. He was 28.

Death-Consciousness in Yoon Dong-ju's Poetry

Death-consciousness is an element constituting the undercurrent of Yoon Dong-ju's poetry. It is an undeniable fact that he was a victim of the age he lived in, and the sudden termination of a poetic genius like his should be regarded as a tragedy caused by the external circumstances that really did not have much bearing upon his inner life as a poet. Close reading of his poetry, however, reveals that his poetic consciousness was heavily charged with the thought of man's mortality, and that not only the fear of untimely death but a transcendental acceptance of it as his fate was ever present in his consciousness throughout his poetic career.

In considering the above issue, we may recall the ancient belief that a poet unwittingly predicts his own fate in the lines he writes. But my aim is not to prove or disprove the validity of such belief. Rather than applying the mystic notion shared by the men of letters in classical literature to the reading of Yoon Dong-ju's poetry, I wish to probe into the nature of the death-consciousness in his poetry and its significance in relation to his lifelong existential search.

It is a well-known fact that Yoon Dong-ju was deeply immersed in the writings of Kierkegaard, whose thoughts became the foundation of existentialism, that important philosophical trend of the twentieth century. Having grown up in a Christian family, Yoon Dong-ju was thus a man torn between the creed of orthodox Christianity and the Kierkegaardian skepticism and distrust of all dogmas. As a poet trying to find a meaning for every moment of his life, Yoon Dong-ju naturally leaned toward existentialism; and, indeed, the whole corpus of his poetic writing may be termed a record of his existential search.

For an existentialist, awareness of one's being alive is the crux of all his thoughts. Awareness of one's being alive, however, presupposes being aware of the truth of mortality. Thus, carrying on a lifelong search for the meaning of his life, Yoon Dong-ju often revealed his deep-rooted death-consciousness in his lines. Here is a poem that clearly shows death-consciousness:

Life and Death

Even today life sang a prelude to death.
When will this song be over?

While we live,
We dance to the song of life, so joyous
That our bones may melt down with it.
While we live, we have no time to think about

> The horror to follow when the song is done—
> When over the hill the sun finally goes down.
>
> Who was it that sang this song,
> Hoping to engrave his name in the sky?
>
> And who was it that stopped singing
> As suddenly as a shower stops?
>
> Those conquerors of death,
> Who have left only their bones!

In this poem, life is seen only as "a prelude to death," and, the poet says: "While we live, we have no time to think about the horror to follow when the song is done." Pointing out that we tend to be forgetful of our mortality while alive is reminding oneself of the futility of all human efforts, including the very act of composing a poem:

> Who was it that sang this song,
> Hoping to engrave his name in the sky?

No one, indeed, can "engrave his name in the sky," no matter how gifted he may be as a poet. But while alive, the poet knows, at the same time, that he has to keep writing, for he is bound to "dance to the song of life." The word 'bones' is used twice in the poem in strikingly different contexts: the self-same bones, which make it possible for us to "dance to the song of life," are not only part of *memento mori* ("Those conquerors of death, who have left only their bones!") but, in truly realistic terms, the only palpable thing we can leave behind, whatever we may try to achieve in our lifetime.

Fully knowing that all human efforts are to turn out to be futile in the presence of the cosmic law of mortality, Yoon Dong-ju still had the aspiration for self-fulfillment. He knew, however, that the end-all result of a lifelong struggle to attain self-fulfillment, indeed for all existential searches, would be only death. The last stanza of *A Confession* is made up of the following lines:

> Then in the mirror looms
> The sad figure of a man
> Walking away under a shooting star.

While struggling to attain self-fulfillment, he could already envision his own self walking toward the realm of death: "walking away under a shooting star." The dichotomy of his psyche—being aware of the truth of mortality (and the consequential nihilism) and the aspiration for self-fulfillment as man and poet—is so poignantly revealed in the following poem:

A Terrible Hour

Who are you calling me there?

In this shade where fallen leaves turn green,
Here I am still breathing.

I have never raised my hand, and
I have no heaven to look up to.

Is there in heaven room for me still,
And are you therefore calling me?

On the morning when I go—after all my work—
The leaves will fall without grieving.

Do not call me yet.

Yoon Dong-ju was a man of split psyche. While clinging to the thought that maturation will come with aging and that self-fulfillment will be finally attained in time, he also had a suppressed longing for the realm of death, of physical annihilation—perhaps because he knew that within the limited time of his life span his existential search would have to come to an end without fruition. The conflict between the two apparently uncompromising aspects of his psyche is well summed up in the following poem:

Returning at Night

As if retreating from the world,

> I return to my small room,
> And turn off the light:
> To leave the light on
> Can be very tiresome,
> For it prolongs the day.
>
> Now I want to open the window
> To let in some fresh air;
> But it is dark outside
> Just like this room,
> Or the world, for that matter;
> The road I took in the rain
> To get back to my room
> Is still wet with the rain.
>
> Unable to wash away
> The mortification of a day,
> I close my eyes—
> When I hear a brook
> Running within me;
> Now my thoughts are ripening
> By themselves, as apples do.

The first stanza of the poem reveals the poet's suppressed death-wish, or longing for a state of forgetfulness. "As if retreating from the world," he returns to his small room—a metaphor for the confined world of his consciousness; and he turns off the light, which only makes him see the physical world:

> To leave the light on
> Can be very tiresome,
> For it prolongs the day.

While withdrawing into the private world of his consciousness, he also wishes "to open the window to let in some fresh air." Here is a collision between the suppressed death-wish and the normal desire to breathe the air of the outside world. But the poet realizes that the outside world—the world of common sense—is only an extension of the world of his consciousness: it is also filled with darkness. The task of bridging the gap between the two—the private world of his consciousness and the world that exists quite independently of his private world—is metaphorically termed "the road I took in the rain to get back to my room," which is "still wet with the rain," the sweat caused by existential anguish. The last stanza contains both resignation ("Unable to wash away the mortification of a day, I close my eyes") and the hope that his thoughts will mature in time:

> When I hear a brook
> Running within me;
> Now my thoughts are ripening
> By themselves, as apples do.

Why did the poet use the simile, "as apples do"? Was he trying to imply that even the fruit of his existential search might turn out to be the cause of another moral downfall comparable to the Biblical one? Yoon Dong-ju was a man of conscience. In using the term "conscience," I do not wish to limit the meaning of the word only to its moral or ethical sense. The word "shame" recurring in his poetry denotes that he was a man obsessed with the idea of attaining the "unity of being" as man and poet. Combined with this sense of obligation for self-fulfillment was the underlying thought of the inherited sin of mankind, a concept deeply rooted in the Christian doctrine. As an existentialist, Yoon Dong-ju thus tried to relieve himself of the burden of admitting the sinful nature of human existence by turning to the notion of God's foreknowledge and the predestination of man's fall:

Primeval Morn (1)

> It was a certain morn—
> A morning not yet tainted
> By spring, summer, autumn, or winter—
>
> When a red flower suddenly bloomed
> In the gleam of the primal sun.
>
> It was the night before—
> Yes, it was the night before—

> That all preparation had been made
>
> To send love along with the snake—
> To let poison grow in a little flower—

Here one notices that the poet has come to terms with the co-existence of good and evil and the essential conflict inherent in human existence. Then, where would a man of ethical scrutiny find a solution for the moral conflict that goes on in his consciousness? Here again the poet's suppressed longing for a state free from the yoke of his physical being reasserts itself:

> *A Wonder*
>
> After pulling off all covering my feet,
> Shall I try to tread on the lake?
> As dusk does, while spreading over it?
>
> Indeed it is a wonder
> That I've been drawn to the lake,
> When no one has called me here.
>
> Today
> Longing, complacency, and envy
> Cling to me like cumbersome medals.
>
> Now I want to have all these
> Washed away in the water;
> Please summon me onto the lake.

The poem sounds like a metaphorical statement of his suppressed death-wish. And one can even note that the poet alludes to the surrealistic feat of Christ, who walked on water. By alluding to one of Christian myths, the poet is projecting himself as a Christ figure, but not with any tinge of presumption. Living in an age that must have been unbearable for a man of sensitivity, Yoon Dong-ju would willingly offer himself as a sacrificial lamb for his compatriots. Thus, in a poem, entitled "The Cross," he prophetically states that he will be happy to die a victim of crucifixion perpetrated by the times:

The Cross

The sunbeams that followed me
Are now hanging on the cross
That soars at the church steeple.

How can one climb up there,
Up to the steeple so high?

Now the bell is not ringing,
I shall loiter awhile, whistling;

And if the cross is granted me,
As it was once to Jesus Christ,
A man who suffered in bliss,

I shall quietly endure,
With my head drooping,
Beneath the darkening sky, while
Blood oozes to bloom like a flower.

It is a prophetic poem, in which the poet already envisions himself as a sacrificial lamb offered on the altar of poesy as well as of patriotic cause. Alluding to his self as a Christ figure is no act of sacrilege or presumption. It is rather an indication of his wish to die a death similar to Christ's.

It may not be doing justice to Yoon Dong-ju's poetry, however, to consider it only as a manifestation of his patriotic zeal or self-imposed sense of mission as one who carried all the burden of human misery. After all, a poet is a private man, who suffers from his own existential agony. Several critics have tried to make him look like a rebel of sorts, by reading his poetry in the political context. But putting what a poetic genius has accomplished in a preconceived mould of historicism is to violate the sanctity of poesy. After all, we must try to listen to the words coming from the depth of a poet's heart—not what he should have sounded like in the schematized canon. The innermost anguish of an existentialist poet, one who had to cope with a Hamletian dilemma, is epitomized in the following poem:

Another Home

The night I came back home,
My bones that followed lay in the self-same bed.

The dark chamber was one with the universe,
And the wind blew down like a voice from heaven.

Looking into the bones
Quietly bleaching in the dark,
I know not whether it is
Myself that weeps, or my bones,
Or my beauteous soul.

The upright dog incorruptible
Barked all night at darkness.
He who barks at darkness
Must be hunting after me.

Let me go away, away,
Like a person pursued,
Unknown to my bones,
To yet another home of peace.

Here Yoon Dong-ju's soul is already in close kinship with death, the *terra incognita*, "from whose bourn no traveler returns." The death-consciousness in Yoon Dong-ju, we note in this poem, has developed into spiritual kinship with death. The "bones that followed" the poet to lie with him "in the self-same bed" become the object of his soul's watching:

Looking into the bones
Quietly bleaching in the dark,
I know not whether it is
Myself that weeps, or my bones,

Or my beauteous soul.

The tripartite division of the poet's self—"myself," "my bones," and "my beauteous soul"—denotes the culmination of an existentialist's search for the real essence of his being. And when the poet longs for the realm of death, "yet another home of peace," the liberation of his soul from his "bones," which have provided the frame of his physical being, is already promised.

The consummation devoutly to be wished, however, is not the annihilation of his physical being. It is neither the perpetual continuation of his poetic spirit, which will "engrave his name in the sky." In a poem, the title of which contains one of Yoon Dong-ju's most beloved words, *Counting the Stars at Night*, the poet both confesses and prophesies:

> Because I have a secret yearning,
> Seated on this star-showered bank,
> I have writ my name thereon,
> And covered it with earth.
>
> In truth, it is because the insects chirp
> All night, and grieve over my bashful name.
>
> But spring shall come to my stars after winter's delay,
> Greening the turf over the graves;
> So, this bank that buries my name
> Shall proudly wear the grass again.

I have not been to the poet's grave yet. But as I pass by the small stone monument raised in his memory in a little grove on the campus of the college where he studied once, I recall the above lines as well as the lines engraved on it:

> *Prologue*
>
> Until I breathe my last breath
> I wish to face my sky without shame.
> Even the wind blowing on leaves
> Has left me restless.

With a heart singing hymns to the stars
I shall love all that must die;
And I shall walk diligently
Upon the path assigned to me.

Tonight again, the stars are blown by the wind.

Watching the young students sitting on the nearby benches, I realize that Yoon Dong-ju still lives in their youthful hearts, and his soul is embedded in one of the stars blown by the wind at night.

Sung-Il Lee

POETRY

Prologue

Until I breathe my last breath
I wish to face my sky without shame.
Even the wind blowing on leaves
Has left me restless.
With a heart singing hymns to the stars
I shall love all that must die;
And I shall walk diligently
Upon the path assigned to me.

Tonight again, the stars are blown by the wind.

Self-Portrait

Turning around the corner of a hill,
I walk alone to the well beside a paddy,
And look inside quietly.

Within the well, the moon is fair,
The clouds flow, the sky stretches,
Blue wind blows, and there is autumn.

And there is a man in it—
Somehow I do not wish to look at him,
And turn my face away to go back.

Walking away, I feel sorry for him;
I go back and look in to see him still there.

I turn away again, not wanting to see him;
While walking away, I start missing him.

Within the well, the moon is fair,
The clouds flow, the sky stretches,
Blue wind blows, and there is autumn;
And a man is there—like memory.

A Boy

Here and there the autumn drifts,
Sad as the withered leaves falling.
Having prepared the spring to return
To each twig whence the leaves fell,
The sky stretches above the tree branches.

The boy intently looks into the sky,
While its blue settles on his brow.
He rubs his warm cheeks with his palms,
And finds they have been tainted in blue.

As he looks into his palms, wondering,
He sees a river flowing therein,
A clear stream along his palm lines;
And within the stream looms a face
Sad as love—Sooni's face.

The boy closes his eyes in rapture;
Yet the river flows on,
Wherein lingers a face—
Sad as love—Sooni's lovely face.

A Snowy Map

This morning, when Sooni is going to leave,
Snow falls in large flakes on my grieving heart,
Covering the map stretched far out of the window.
The room is empty, for I am alone.
The walls and the ceiling are all white—
Is it snowing even in this room?

Are you going indeed—as someone of the past?
What I wanted to say before you leave
I would write in a letter, but cannot post it,
Not knowing where you are going, where you will live,
In what street, in what village, under which roof—
Is my heart the only address I know?

I cannot follow your small footsteps on the snow,
For snow keeps falling, covering all.
When this snow melts,
On each step you leave, a flower will bloom.
When I look for your footsteps among the flowers,
In my heart there will be a yearlong snowfall.

Returning at Night

As if retreating from the world,
I return to my small room,
And turn off the light:
To leave the light on
Can be very tiresome,
For it prolongs the day.

Now I want to open the window
To let in some fresh air;
But it is dark outside
Just like this room,
Or the world, for that matter;
The road I took in the rain
To get back to my room
Is still wet with the rain.

Unable to wash away
The mortification of a day,
I close my eyes—
When I hear a brook
Running within me;
Now my thoughts are ripening
By themselves, as apples do.

At a Hospital

Lying in the backyard of the hospital, with her face hidden in the shade of an apricot tree, a young woman is doing sunbathing, with her white legs exposed below her white gown. Till the day wanes, no one, not even a butterfly, comes to visit her, who is known to suffer from an ailment in her chest. Around the indifferent apricot-tree boughs not even the wind tarries.

I myself have visited this hospital for the first time, no longer able to stand the chest pain I have felt long. But my old doctor cannot diagnose a young man's illness; he says I am not ill. Ah, this unbearable suffering, this extreme fatigue! But I must not get angry.

The woman gets up, tidies herself, and after adorning her chest with a marigold plucked from the flower-garden, walks away toward the ward. Wishing her to regain good health—well, me, too—I lie down on the spot where she lay awhile ago.

A New Road

Across the brook, then to the wood—
Across the hill, then to the village—

My road runs on, a road ever new,
I took yesterday and will take today,

Where dandelions bloom, and magpies fly,
Where girls tread on, and the wind blows.

My road runs on, a road ever new,
As it does today, and will tomorrow.

Across the brook, then to the wood—
Across the hill, then to the village—

A Street without Signboards

As you step down on the platform,
You won't see anybody around.

There are only visitors,
Only those who look like visitors;

Since no house bears a signboard,
No need to worry about finding one.

With no letters glittering
In the multifarious colors
Of red and blue,

Every nook and corner of the street
Is brightened by an old gaslight lamp
That emanates benevolent beams.

As they grab one another's wrist,
They are all kind neighbors,
All of them with warm hearts.

Spring, summer, autumn, winter
Move along, taking turns smoothly.

Primeval Morn (1)

It was a certain morn—
A morning not yet tainted
By spring, summer, autumn, or winter—

When a red flower suddenly bloomed
In the gleam of the primal sun.

It was the night before—
Yes, it was the night before—
That all preparation had been made

To send love along with the snake—
To let poison grow in a little flower—

Primeval Morn (2)

Where the snow lies white,
Over the howling telegraph poles,
The voice of God is heard.

What revelation?

With haste,
When spring comes round,
Will I enact my sin,
And wake to pangs in store.

And after Eve's travail and toil,

Hiding my shame with fig leaves,

I will endure the sweat on my brow.

(Translated by Insoo Lee, *The Seoul Times*, December 24, 1948)

Till Dawn Breaks

Wrap in black garments
Those who are dying slowly;

Dress up in white clothes
Those who are still living;

Then upon the same beds
Let them lie side by side to sleep.

If they burst into crying,
Soothe them with human milk.

When soon dawn breaks,
A trumpet sound will be heard.

A Terrible Hour

Who are you calling me there?

In this shade where fallen leaves turn green,
Here I am still breathing.

I have never raised my hand, and
I have no heaven to look up to.

Is there in heaven room for me still,
And are you therefore calling me?

On the morning when I go—after all my work—
The leaves will fall without grieving.

Do not call me yet.

The Cross

The sunbeams that followed me
Are now hanging on the cross
That soars at the church steeple.

How can one climb up there,
Up to the steeple so high?

Now the bell is not ringing,
I shall loiter awhile, whistling;

And if the cross is granted me,
As it was once to Jesus Christ,
A man who suffered in bliss,

I shall quietly endure,
With my head drooping,
Beneath the darkening sky, while
Blood oozes to bloom like a flower.

Wind Blows

Whence is the wind coming,
And whereto is it going?

While the wind blows,
I suffer for no reason.

Do I suffer for no reason, indeed?

Neither have I loved a woman,
Nor have I grieved for the times.

While the wind keeps blowing,
I stand firmly upon a rock.

While the river flows on,
I am standing upon a hill.

A Sad People

White kerchiefs cover their black hair,
White rubber slippers their cracked toes.

White jackets and skirts hide their sad trunks,
White cloth-bands tie up their slender waists.

Walk with Your Eyes Closed

Dear children, who adore the sun,
Dear children, who love the stars,

Now in the dark of the night
Walk with your eyes closed.

As you walk, after each step
Strew the seeds in your hands.

If you get tripped on a stone,
Open your eyes wide, quickly.

Another Home

The night I came back home,
My bones that followed lay in the self-same bed.

The dark chamber was one with the universe,
And the wind blew down like a voice from heaven.

Looking into the bones
Quietly bleaching in the dark,
I know not whether it is
Myself that weeps, or my bones,
Or my beauteous soul.

The upright dog incorruptible
Barked all night at darkness.
He who barks at darkness
Must be hunting after me.

Let me go away, away,
Like a person pursued,
Unknown to my bones,
To yet another home of peace.

(Translated by Insoo Lee, *The Seoul Times*, May 18, 1948)

The Road

I have lost something.
Not knowing what I have lost and where,
Groping my pockets with my both hands,
I walk out to be on the road.

The road runs along a wall
That stretches on a long line of stone-pile.

With its iron gate firmly closed,
The wall casts a long shadow on the road;

And the road runs on—
From morning to evening,
From evening to morning;

I grope the wall with tears in my eyes,
And then turn my eyes up to the sky
That baffles me with its infinite blue.

I keep walking on this bare road, for
I am still on the other side of the wall.

I live on from day to day, for
I am still looking for what I have lost.

Counting the Stars at Night

Up where the seasons pass,
The sky is filled with autumn.

In this untroubled quietude
I could almost count these autumn-couched stars.

But why I cannot now enumerate
Those one or two stars in my breast
Is because the dawn is breaking soon,
And I have tomorrow night in store,
And because my youth is not yet done.

Memory for one star,
Love for another star,
Sorrow for another star,
Longing for another star,
Poetry for another star,
And O Mother! for another star.

Mother, I try to call each star by some such evocative word, names of school children with whom I shared desks, names of alien girls like Pae, Kyong, Ok, names of maidens who have already become mothers, names of neighbors who lived in poverty, names of birds and beasts like pigeon, puppy, rabbit, donkey, deer, and names of poets like Francis Jammes and Rainer Maria Rilke.

They are as far away
And intangible as the stars.

Mother,
You too are in the distant land of Manchuria.

Because I have a secret yearning,
Seated on this star-showered bank,

I have writ my name thereon,
And covered it with earth.

In truth, it is because the insects chirp
All night, and grieve over my bashful name.

But spring shall come to my stars after winter's delay,
Greening the turf over the graves;
So, this bank that buries my name
Shall proudly wear the grass again.

(Translated by Insoo Lee, *The Seoul Times*, December 23, 1948)

White Shadows

Standing at a corner of the dusky road,
I strain my day-weary ears
To listen to the dusk carry its steps.

Was I born so gifted as to
Hear the footsteps of dusk?

Now I have understood all, alas, too late,
I send away one by one
My innumerable selves that have suffered long,
To where they are due;
Then, into the dark around the corner
My white shadows walk away silently.

These dim white shadows—
The long-cherished shadows of mine!

After sending all my shadows away,
I return, empty-hearted, through an alley,
To my room slowly sinking into dusk,

Where I shall stay calm and peaceful—
Like a lamb indulging in daylong grazing.

A Beloved Memory

One morning, when spring was coming,
I was standing at a small station in Seoul,
To wait for the train, like hope or love.

I was casting a thin shadow
Upon the platform, smoking.

My shadow blew the shadow of smoke,
And the pigeons flew, unashamed of
The inside of their wings exposed to the sun.

The train, bringing no new hope,
Only carried me far.

The spring is gone now—
In a quiet rented room in a foreign land
I long for myself—like hope or love—
The one I left behind at home.

Several trains, bringing no one,
Must have passed by already today.

Even now he must be loitering
Upon the hill near the station—
Waiting for one, who is not coming.

—Ah, youth, stay there long.

A Flowing Street

Blurring my vision, the fog flows on. The street also seems to flow. Whereto are that tramcar, the automobiles, and all the vehicles running on their wheels, being swept in the flow? Without a harbor for setting an anchor, bearing many pitiful people, the city flows along with the fog.

As I stand, laying my hands on the red mailbox at a street corner, the street lamps faintly glimmer, while everything flows. What does it symbolize that they refuse to be put out? My dear friends, Park and Kim! Where are you now, while the fog flows endlessly?

"On a new day's morning, let's hold our hands together fondly again." After dropping this brief message in the mailbox, I keep vigil all night, waiting for a postman to appear like a giant, wearing a uniform decorated with a gold badge and glittering with gold buttons. What a welcome visitor the morning will bring!

Throughout this night, the fog flows on.

A Poem Written Easily

The night rain whispers outside the window
Of this small rented room in a foreign land.

Knowing that a poet is a creature of sad fate,
Shall I write a few lines to compose a poem?

Having received money sent from home
That brings the smell of sweat and love,

With a college notebook stuck under my arm,
I go to class to attend an old professor's lecture.

Having lost my childhood friends,
All of them, one after another,

What am I still trying to accomplish,
While sinking in the stream of life?

When living a life is hard, as they say,
To write verses with ease is a shame.

In a small rented room in a foreign land,
While the night rain whispers outside,

I turn on the light to push out the dark a little,
And wait for the morning to come like an age.

I offer myself a small hand—
For the first handshake that brings tears and comfort.

Spring (1)

Spring flows like a rivulet in my bloodstream;
On the hill near the warbling brook bloom
Forsythias, azaleas, yellow cabbage flowers.

Having lived through the cold winter,
I, too, grow green like grass.

You, merry larks,
Soar up in jubilee from any furrow.

The blue sky stretching above
Looks so high, dizzying an onlooker.

A Confession

In the copper mirror rusty green,
My face lingers
Like a sad relic
Of an ancient kingdom.

My contrition is condensed in a single line:
—"For twenty-four years and a month
   What futile expectations have kept me alive?"

On a joyful day, tomorrow or the day after,
I shall add a line of repentance:
—"On that day when I was still young,
   Why did I make such a shameful confession?"

Night after night, my mirror
I wipe with my palms and soles;

Then in the mirror looms
The sad figure of a man
Walking away under a shooting star.

Liver

Upon the sunlit rock at seashore,
Let me spread my liver to dry it up.

Like a rabbit that ran away from Mount Caucasus,
Let me turn round and round, guarding my liver.

You, hungry vulture that I've raised for long,
Come and devour it, no need to hurry.

You need to fatten yourself;
And I must languish to become lean and gaunt.

But you, turtle,
I will not be coaxed by the treacherous offer
You once brought from the palace of the deep.

Prometheus, poor Prometheus,
Ah, for your rebellious act of stealing fire,
You are endlessly sinking down
With the rock hung on your neck.

Translator's Note:
The poem contains allusions to the myth of Prometheus, who is bound to a rock of Mount Caucasus and gets his liver devoured by the vultures as punishment for having stolen fire from Olympus to bring it to men, and the Korean folktale involving a rabbit that was coaxed by a turtle, a messenger of the palace of the deep. The ruler of the deep needed the liver of a rabbit to have his illness cured; so he dispatched a turtle to land to bring a rabbit. The rabbit was coaxed to follow the turtle to the underwater world; but, realizing that it had been tricked by the turtle, the rabbit told the turtle that it had left its liver behind. So they returned to land to bring the liver. But when they came out of the water, the rabbit ridiculed the turtle, saying it had paid back for the treachery of the turtle with its wit.

Sleepless Nights

One, two, three, four,
. . . .
So many nights—
Too many to count.

Consolation

A spider, with its insidious intent, drew a web in the backyard of the hospital, between the railings and the flowerbed, where people's feet rarely reach, to the full view of the young man in need of fresh air to watch, lying.

A butterfly flying unto the flowerbed got entangled in the web. No matter how hard the butterfly fluttered its yellow wings, it only got entangled more and more. The spider rapidly went to it, and wound up its whole body with its endless gossamer. The man made a deep sigh.

A word that can console the man, who has gotten his illness after much toil and trouble hard to bear for a man of his age— Well, there was none, except sweeping off the web.

Eightfold Blessing
—From *St. Matthew*, Chapter 5, 3–12—

Blessed are they that mourn,
Blessed are they that mourn,
Blessed are they that mourn,
Blessed are they that mourn,
Blessed are they that mourn,
Blessed are they that mourn,
Blessed are they that mourn,
Blessed are they that mourn,

For they shall mourn for ever.

Mountain Water

One who suffers long and alone!
Even along the ripples on his sleeves
A rivulet flows, warbling in his heart.
There is none to share a talk tonight,
Nor can he sing along amidst the street noise.
Like a picture drawn,
He is sitting beside a brook.
Entrusting love and work to the street,
Let him go silently to the sea,
Let him head toward the sea.

An Ailing Rose

As the rose is ailing,
I can't send it to any of my neighbors.

Shall I put it in a hooded wagon, so that
It may ride alone till it reaches a mountain?

Or shall I put it in a steamboat
Sadly whistling for a voyage to an ocean?

Or shall I put it on a plane with propellers
Roaring loudly to fly to the stratosphere?

None of these choices
By no means seems feasible.

Before my toddler boy wakes from his dream,
I shall bury the flower in my bosom.

Like the Moon

On a silent night when the moon grows,
The way annual rings grow,
Love as lonely as the moon
Blooms in my aching heart,
The way annual rings grow.

The Pepper Patch

Revealing its flesh so red
Deep in the withering leaves,
Peppers ripen in the hot sun,
Like girls in their full bloom.

Holding a basket in her hand,
Grandma lingers on the patch;
And the thumb-sucking child,
Toddling about, follows grandma.

Cosmos

The clean-looking cosmos
Is my only dear lady.

When the moon shines chilly,
I walk to the cosmos garden,
Unable to suppress my longing
For the girl dear to my memory.

The cosmos becomes shy
At the chirping of the crickets;

And, standing before the cosmos,
I become shy as when a young boy.

The cosmos and I share one heart,
For, though twain, we are one.

A Portrait of My Younger Brother

As cold moonbeam is cast on his ruddy brow,
My younger brother's face is a sad portrait.

I stop walking,
And holding his small hand, ask him:
—"What do you want to be, when you grow up?"
—"Why, a man."
His answer is terse and tart.

I let go his hand,
And look into his face again.

As pale moonlight bathes his brow,
Indeed, his face is a sad portrait.

A Wonder

After pulling off all covering my feet,
Shall I try to tread on the lake,
As dusk does, while spreading over it?

Indeed it is a wonder
That I've been drawn to the lake,
When no one has called me here.

Today
Longing, complacency, and envy
Cling to me like cumbersome medals.

Now I want to have all these
Washed away in the water;
Please summon me onto the lake.

The Temple of Love

Dear Sooni, when was it that you entered my temple?
When was it that I entered yours?

Our temple is the temple of love,
Wherein has settled an ancient custom.

Dear Sooni, close your crystal eyes like a doe;
I'll tidy up my hair bushy like a lion's mane.

Our love was of the mute.

Before the flame on the sacred candle-holder dies,
Run away quickly, Sooni, through the front gate.

Before darkness and wind crash into our window,
I'll walk away far through the back gate,
Having our eternal love enshrined in my heart.

Now a tranquil lake in a forest is waiting for you;
Rugged and precipitous mountains will face me.

A Rainy Night

Roar and crash!
The sound of the waves shatters on the window pane,
And my dream in a sweet slumber disperses.

My sleep becomes disturbed, as if by thronging whales,
And there is no way to have it restored.

I turn on light, and having readjusted my sleepwear,
Offer an earnest prayer in the middle of the night.

Fearing my cherished town may get flooded again,
I feel more anxiety than my usual longing for the sea.

A Dying Man's Wish

In the bleak empty room
A dying man's lips move, but no sound:

"My son left home to collect pearls. My first son,
They say, has fallen in love with a diving girl.
Look out to see if he's coming tonight."

A father, who suffered lifelong loneliness, dies;
Upon his closing eyes a shade of grief is cast.

Somewhere near the lonesome hut a dog barks,
While the moon throws bright beams on its door.

Window

At each break between classes
I walk to the window.

—The window has a live lesson to give.

Please make a strong fire in the stove,
For the classroom is fraught with chill.

Now a yellow leaf falls, spinning,
Perhaps a small whirlwind is blowing.

Even so, as the bright sunrays
Shower on the cold window,
I wait for the school bell to ring.

An Afternoon in a Glen

My song sounds hollow
Like a sad mountain echo.

My shadow
Cast on the valley lane
Only reflects my pitiful figure.

Meditation in an afternoon
Only leads me to drowsiness.

Piro Peak

Looking down over
The panoramic view,

I cannot help that
My knees tremble.

The white birches
Look prematurely old.

The birds in flight
Look like butterflies.

Clouds turn into rain,
To prove what they say.

Clothes flapping in the wind
Make me feel even colder.

Note: 'Piro' is the highest peak of Mount Kŭm-gang, famous for its scenic beauty and grandeur.

The Sea

The wind that carries and sprays
Water drops is cool and refreshing.

Every branch of the pine trees is
Turning away, as if in petulance,

Pushing one another
Only to be pushed in return.

The waves crossing the ridges
Raise foam, as waterfalls do.

Children run and gather ashore,
And dip their hands in water.

The sadness of the sea deepens,
As the seagulls shriek louder.

The sea I leave behind today,
Looking back over and again!

Pensive Moment

Bushy hair covers my head like roof-thatch;
Whistling wind aggrieved tickles my nose.

As my eyes remain closed lightly like windows,
Longing seeps into me like darkness tonight.

Pathos

Following the moon of the desolate century,
I wish to stroll on a field, unknown yet familiar.

Having rushed out at a wee hour,
As if sprung up from my bed,
I may be gripped by much solitude,
As I walk on a boundless plain alone.

Ah, this young man, that I am, will be
No less sad than a pyramid on a desert.

Downpour

Now my eyes dazzle and ears are numb,
Lightning must've struck a distant town.

From the sky covered by an ink tray
Rain falls like arrows pouring down thick.

My yard as small as a palm spread
Easily turns into a lake murky like my mood.

The wind spins like a top;
The trees can't keep their heads upright.

Receiving my reverent mood like a guest,
I gulp a mouthful of what pours from Noah's heaven.

That Woman

That apple that first ripened
When flowers bloomed together
Fell to the earth first.

Even today
Autumn wind keeps blowing.

That red apple
That fell on the roadside
A passerby picked up on his way.

Thermometer

A thermometer hanging by neck on a cold marble pillar—
With a short slender mercury column to be seen through,
Its heart is purer than the transparent glass encasing it.

With a simple vein, it is easily swept by public opinion;
Often swallowing cold saliva spouting like a fountain
Against its will, it wastes its energy.

August schoolyard surrounded by sunflowers in full bloom
Is preferable than the cold room of Sudol's house in winter,
Where its finger has to point to below zero—
Ah, that day when all blood will seethe!

"There was a big shower yesterday, but it is sunny today.
You may walk to the hill or the wood, wearing a light jacket."

So I whispered to myself, inaudible to others,
Not even aware that I was so doing.

Perhaps, following the season of a truthful century,
Running out of the fence that hides all but the sky,
I'll have to keep my position put on me like history.

Landscape

The green sea with the spring wind on its back
Looks like being ready to pour out any moment.

The waves bouncing like pleated skirts blown up
Look pleasantly light, as if ready to shatter.

At the top of the mast a red flag flaps
Like a woman's hair in the wind.

With this lively landscape ahead or behind,
I feel like strolling about all day long,

Bearing a gloomy sky above on a day in May,
Toward a hill embroidered in the hue of the sea.

Moonlit Night

Pushing the white wave of the moonbeam,
Treading the shadows of the withered trees,
I walk to a cemetery with heavy footsteps,
While sadness fills my heart befriending loneliness.

Nobody is at the mound where someone ought to be,
And quietude pervades, drenched in the waving moonlight.

Market

Early in the morning, women gather to the market,
With basketful of their careworn, weary life,
Carrying it on their heads, backs, and shoulders;
They keep gathering there, armful and handful.

To spread their poor life row after row,
They swarm in and out, like ebb and flow;
They bellow and yell and argue, each for life.

All day long they measure their petty living with
Bowls and scales and rulers for small gains
Till a day of peddling is over, and then return home,
Carrying the remnant of what sustains their bitter life.

Night

The donkey in the pen brays out, loud and long.
At the noise, the baby wakes, bursting into cry.
The oil-lamp bears a small flame on its wick.

The father feeds the donkey with a bundle of hay.
The mother lets the baby suck her nipple awhile.
Then the night falls into quiet sleep again.

Twilight Turns into a Sea

Another day languidly sinks down
Into a dark, blue stretch of waves.

How is it that a throng of black fish
Crosses the sea dyed in the color of ink?

Sea plants turned into drifting leaves!
Each of the sea plants looks sad.

A clear seascape drawn on my west window!
The sorrow of an orphan chewing breast-tie!

Now with the heart of a first voyager,
I lie down on the floor and roll on it.

Twilight turns into a sea
To make numberless ships launch into it
And embark on a voyage together with me.

Morning

Swishing and whirling,
The cow's tail, like a soft whip,
Chases off darkness,
And finally brings a bright morning.

Now the morning of this village
Swells like a well-fed cow's haunch.
The villagers, who feed on bean porridge,
Kept the summer nurtured on their sweat.

On each grass blade dangle sweat drops.

This healthy and wholesome morning
I breathe in deeply, over and again.

An Autumn Night

On an autumn night,
When dreary rain falls,
I rush out of the room
Without wearing anything,
And crouching on the stepping panel,
Shoot out urine,
The way a child does.

Washed Clothes Hung over a String

An afternoon when washed clothes whisper,
With their legs hanging down from a string—

The dazzling bright sunrays of July quietly
Fall on the trim and tidy-looking clothes only.

A Road in the Valley

Mountains keep running in two rows,
And the rushes roar in hoarse voice.
Midsummer sun riding on the clouds
Is about to cross the vale in haste.

Along the ridges rise small rocks
Rugged as the horns on a calf's head;
And, like the velvety hair of a brindled cow,
Plants grow thick and green on the ridges.

The footsteps of a wayfarer returning home
To the vale after three years' sojourn away
Stomp on the ground, as he plods on,
Like a crane with featherless legs.

A worn sandal dangling from his stick
Slung over his shoulder moves to and fro,
And a magpie flies, carrying food for its brood.
Otherwise, the vale is as serene as the plodder.

Chickens (1)

Yon over the shabby coop spreads the blue sky.
But the chickens oblivious of their inborn freedom
Keep chattering about their careworn life,
And scream about the labor involved in production.

Swarming out of the gloomy coop
Are the chickens of foreign origin— Leghorn!
Sometimes there are fine afternoons in March,
When from a school a flock of birds pour out.

Digging the manure melting wet and swampy,
The chickens keep moving their graceful legs;
And hunger forces their beaks to remain busy,
Till their eyes become blurred, turning all red.

Forest

As the ticktack of the clock beats my shrinking heart,
I hear the forest calling me drowning in anxiety.

The dark forest knit with a millennium's annual rings
Is ready to take in and hug a world-weary one.

From above the black waves of the forest
Darkness weighs down on a young heart,

And the evening wind shaking the leaves
Blows on to make me tremble with fear.

The distant croaking of the frogs in early summer
Evokes my memory of an old village where I lived.

Only the stars twinkling through the trees
Lead me to a hope for the coming days.

The Sunlit Side

Spring wind bearing the dust of this land blows there,
Swirling like a spinning wheel of the Chinese people;

And the soft touch of the variegated rays of April sun
Each sorrowful one feels, as he stands before a wall behind.

Two children absorbed in the game of land-taking
Are agitated over the span of each one's small hand!*

Oh, no! I fear lest
Peace so fragile might be shattered any minute.

---

* The poem depicts the tragic situation incurred by poverty-stricken people's migration across the border between Korea and China. Korean trespassers of the Chinese territory in Manchuria were often executed. The poet compares this bleak historical fact with children's game of land-taking. Children drew a circle on the ground, and each in turn flipped a dice-size pebble. If the pebble hit his opponent's, he spread his palm to the full, thereby claiming that portion covered by his palm as his new acquisition of the land.

Mountain Top

Now that I have come up to the mountain top,
The streets look like the lines on a *baduk** board,
And the river looks like a baby snake creeping.
Even now people must be scattered about
Like *baduk* stones on the line-drawn board.

The midday sun
Glitters only on the tin roofs,
And a train crawling slowly
Stops at the station, and puffing out
Black smoke, starts moving again.

For fear that the sky spread like a canopy
Might collapse, covering all the streets,
I feel like climbing even higher.

---

* 'Baduk' is a game two people play on a board with lines drawn crisscross by putting small pebbles separated into black and white on the spots where the drawn lines cross. Innumerable pebbles can be used by the two game players. Winning at the game is decided by the number of the squares obtained.

Chest (1)

A soundless drum—
When I feel stuffy,
I beat my chest with my fist.

Nonetheless,
"Hoo—"
A deep sigh is much better.

Chest (2)

Winter night is deepening, while
I hug the pot with no fire burning.

My heart with only ashes within trembles
To hear the wind that rattles the window-pane.

Twilight

Stealing in between the sliding doors,
Sunlight draws a long line, and erases it.

Over the roofs, a flock of crows fly
By twos, threes, and fours, constantly,
To the north sky, swiftly and writhing.

As for me,
I feel like flying in the northern sky.

Southern Sky

The swallow has two wings.
A chilly autumn day—

A frosty evening,
When one longs for Mom's breast—
A young soul on the single wing of nostalgia
Only hovers around in the southern sky—

Dream Has Shattered

Dream opened its eyes,
In the deep, dark mist—

The singing lark
Has flown away;

No golden grass, where
Spring songs overflowed.

The tower has crumbled,
The tower of a red heart—

The marble tower carved with fingernails
The storm of one evening destroyed utterly.

O, a field of devastation,
Tears and a choked throat!

Dream has shattered;
The tower has crumbled.

On Such a Day

The day when the flag of five colors and the flag of the sun[*]
Dance each on the two friendly stone columns of the front gate,
Children of the region with a line drawn played merrily.

On the children wearied of the tiresome subjects of a day
Settled languor and boredom not to blame,
And they were too simple and too naïve
To understand what 'contradiction' meant.

On such a day as this
I wish to call my hardheaded brother
I have lost.

---

[*] "The 'flag of five colors' was the flag of 'the Empire of Manchuria,' a colony of Japan, and the 'flag of the sun' the flag of 'the Empire of Japan.' On a national holiday, the two flag were hung on gate, one on each of the gate-poles, respectively.

Soccer Field in the Afternoon

Late spring, the awaited Saturday—
The Kyung-sung bound train of 3:30 PM
Has passed by, vomiting thick smoke of coal.

The ball strong enough to pull a body
Has lost its magnetic power;
And one gulp of water
Is enough to moisten throat
That burns with thirst.
Young heart feels rapid flow of blood,
While iron legs turn weak in languor.

Along with the black smoke of the train,
The blue mountain sinks down
Well far over the haze yonder.

Lark

The lark doesn't care for the back lane
That has turned muddy in early spring.
It likes to sing hilarious songs,
With its light wings widespread,
While it soars up unto the bright open sky.
But I, even today,
Dragging a pair of punctured shoes,
Wander through the backstreets,
Like a miserable small fish.
Is it because I'm deprived of wings and songs
That I feel stuffy in my chest?

Upon Moran Peak

Over the slender twigs of the pines
Skims the wing of the warm breeze,
And on the Daedong River with ice floating
Midday sunbeams glide.

At the site of the ruin of an old castle,
Innocent little girls hop around,
Chattering in a foreign tongue
Probably they themselves don't know.

What a churlish thing, that automobile!

Meal Ticket

The meal ticket provides three meals a day.

The kitchen lady gives to the youngsters
Three white bowls all at once:

One for soup boiled with Daedong River water,
One for steamed rice grown in Pyong-an-do field,
And one saucer with hot pepper bean paste of Chosŏn.

The meal ticket makes our bellies full and round.

Bidding Farewell

The day when snow melts to turn into water,
Hazy fog fills the gray sky, and
The large locomotive shrieks sharp and loud,
Inducing a small heart to throb and pound.

Farewell is too rushed, and causes pain in heart.
Having promised to meet the one I love
At the place where we work together,
I watch the train turn round the corner of the hill
Before my hand cools and tears dry up in my eyes.

Pigeons

On this bright Sunday morning when sky is so clear,
Seven pretty mountain pigeons
Making one feel like hugging
Are pecking grains competitively,
Exchanging incomprehensible dialogue,
On the empty paddy newly cropped for harvest.

Stirring the quiet air with their neat wings,
Two of them fly away.
Perhaps they remembered the squabs at home.

Firmament

On that summer day
The passionate poplar
Spread its arms and waved them
To grope on the blue breast of the sky
Ready to descend on the small shady spot
The burning sun had spared.

Beneath the sky spread like a canopy,
The dancing clouds fled to the south,
Leading the shower and the lightning
That had been lingering around.
The lofty blue firmament
Spreads above the branches as in a picture,
And has invited the round moon and the geese,
Asking them to come and join.

A well-fed young heart burns in aspiration,
And on an autumn day full of longing
Scorns tears shed in dejection.

Daydreaming

Daydreaming—
A tower of my heart—
I build this tower in silence.
In the firmament of glory and vanity,
Not fearing that it may crumble,
I build it up layer on layer.

The infinite stretch of my daydreaming—
That is an ocean within my heart—
Spreading my two arms wide,
I swim freely and to my heart's content
In the ocean of my heart
To the horizon stretched to golden learning.

On the Street

The street in the moonlit night—
A thoroughfare of the Northern land,
Where wind blows like mad—
Like a small mermaid I swim
Under the street lamp,
That is the pearl of a city.
Lit by the moon and the street lamp,
I cast two or three shadows
That grow bigger or smaller.

As I walk on the street of pain,
The ash-gray street at night,
Within my heart there blows
A gush of wind gyrating.
Though drowned in loneliness,
My mind sends out its shadow
Layer after layer like petals shed.
Bluish imagination floats high,
And then sinks down low.

There's No Such a Thing as Tomorrow
—A Child's Observation

People kept talking about tomorrow;
So I asked them what it is.
They said: "Tomorrow will be
When night is gone and dawn comes."

Anxiously waiting for a new day,
I slept through the night and woke up
To learn that tomorrow was no more—
It was another today.

Friends,
There is no such a thing as tomorrow.

Life and Death

Even today life sang a prelude to death.
When will this song be over?

While we live,
We dance to the song of life, so joyous
That our bones may melt down with it.
While we live, we have no time to think about
The horror to follow when the song is done—
When over the hill the sun finally goes down.

Who was it that sang this song,
Hoping to engrave his name in the sky?

And who was it that stopped singing
As suddenly as a shower stops?

Those conquerors of death,
Who have left only their bones!

That Single Candle

That single candle—
I smell its scent permeating my room.

Before the altar of light crumbled down,
I saw that pure sacrificial offering on it.

Its body reminding one of a goat's rib bone,
Along with its wick, the core of its life,
Melts down, as it burns itself,
While it sheds jade-like tears and blood.

Even then, glimmering on my desk,
The candle dances like a fairy lady.

I smell the solemn scent of the offering
That permeates my room, after darkness
Has run away through a hole in the window,
The way a pheasant flees, seeing a falcon.

Echo

A magpie croaked;
Echo answered.
None heard
That echo.

But the magpie heard
That echo.
It alone heard
That echo.

The Cricket and I

A cricket and I
Chatted, sitting on a grassy lawn together.

We chirred and chirped.
We chirped and chirred.

The cricket and I made a firm pledge
That none but two of us should know.

We chirred and chirped.
We chirped and chirred.

A cricket and I
Pledged that night, when the moon was bright.

Dawn Comes with the Baby's Crying

There's no rooster at our home.
But when the baby starts crying,
Asking for milk,
Dawn comes.

There's no clock at our home.
But when the baby starts whining,
Asking for milk,
Dawn comes.

Sunflower's Face

My sister's face is a sunflower's:
Soon after the sun rises, she goes to work.

The sunflower's face is my sister's:
She returns home with a drooping face.

Sunlight and Wind

With a finger wet with saliva
I poke in the paper screen
To make a hole,
So that I can watch Mom
Go to the market-place.

A morning bright with sunlight,

With a finger wet with saliva
I poke in the paper screen
To make another hole,
So that I can see Mon
Return from the market-place.

An evening cool as breeze blows.

Trees

As the trees dance,
    Wind blows;
As the trees remain calm,
    Wind sleeps.

Mandol

On his way home from school,
Near a telegraph pole
Mandol picked up five pebbles.

Aiming at the telegraph pole,
He threw the first pebble:
"Yes, hit!"
He threw the second:
"Hew! Not hit!"
He threw the third:
"Yes, hit!"
He threw the fourth:
"Heck! Not hit!"
He threw the fifth:
"Yes, hit!"

"Three out of five. . . .
That's good enough!
At tomorrow's exam,
If I hit three out of five—
No matter how hard I try
To finish 'nine times nine' counting,
Every time I get only sixty points.
What the heck! Let me go kick the ball."

Next day, what do you think?
Do you think Mandol turned in
A blank sheet of paper to his teacher,

Or, he received sixty points
In the exam he took next morning?

Grandpa

How come you insist
That the rice-cake is sweet,
When it tastes bitter for sure?

Firefly Light

Let's go, let's go,
Let's go to the wood.
To pick up the pieces of the moon,
Let's go to the wood.

The fireflies on a month's last night
Are the pieces of the moon shattered.

Let's go, let's go,
Let's go to the wood.
To pick up the pieces of the moon,
Let's go to the wood.

Both

The sea is blue;
So is the sky.

The sea is boundless;
So is the sky.

When I throw a stone into the sea,
It only smiles at me.

When I spit onto the sky,
It remains quiet.

What a Lie!

"Knock, knock, knock!
Open the door, please!
Let me stay just over a night!"
    "The night is deep, and it's bitter cold.
    Who can it be?"
I open the door only to find
That a black dog has deceived me,
Wagging its tail and hitting the door.

"Quack, quack, quack!
I've laid eggs!
Wench, pick them up in hurry!"
    The girl rushes to the coop
    Only to find out that it was a lie.
That darn bitch of a hen
Made a flagrant lie,
While the sun still shines bright.

Pockets

The two pockets
Worried about having
Nothing to be filled,

Once winter comes,
Feel stuffy with two fists tucked in.

Winter

Underneath the eaves
Are hung dried radish leaves,
Rustling with crisp sound,
As they shiver in the cold.

On the pavement
The round drops of horse shit
Get frozen to turn into lumps
To send out bell-like ringing.

Chickens (2)

Endowed with big wings,
Why can't chickens fly?

Engrossed in digging the earth,
They must've forgotten how to fly.

Snow (1)

Having fallen
So white and bounteously,
Snow cannot remember
How it has piled up so high.

Apple

One single red apple
Four of us,
Father, mother, sister, and I,
Ate it all, without peeling its skin,
Till we've devoured its core.

Snow (2)

Last night
Snow fell softly and sumptuously.

It fell to cover
The roofs,
The roads, the paddies,
For fear that they may feel cold.

That's why
It falls only in the cold winter.

Pattern for Footwear

Mother,
Why do you save the sheets that my sister
Throws away after practicing calligraphy?

Oh, I didn't know
That you put my footwear on them
To draw lines on them
And set up the pattern for my footwear.

Mother,
Why do you keep and save
The pencil stubs I throw away?

Oh, I didn't know that you use them,
Wetting their tips with saliva,
To draw lines on cloth,
And set up the lines for my footwear.

A Letter

Sister!
This winter again
Snow has fallen a whole lot.

Shall I mail to you
A white envelope
Containing a handful of snow,
With no writings in it,
Bearing no stamp on it,
Clean as it looks?

For in that land where you went,
I've heard that no snow falls.

A Dog

A dog is running
   on the snow,
Drawing a flower
   on the snow.

Sparrows

The yard where autumn passed over is white paper,
Upon which sparrows practice how to draw letters.

Repeating the sound of each letter with their chirrup,
They practice drawing the letters with their toes.

Though they practice drawing letters all day long,
The only letter they scrawl is what sounds, "Chirrup!"

Spring (2)

Our baby breathes softly, asleep
At the warm corner of the room.

The cat lets out its purring snore,
Lying on the mud-built kettle seat.

Baby-like soft breeze blows down
From the slender branches of a tree.

Uncle-like sun pours bright beams
From the middle of the clear sky.

What Do They Eat to Live?

People at seashore
Catch fish to eat and live.

People in deep mountains
Dig potatoes to bake and eat.

What about those in the stars?
Do they eat anything, at all?

Chimney

From the low chimney of the mountain hut
Why does smoke rise in fine daylight hour?

Must be that a bunch of young men are sitting
Around fire, blinking their black eyes, while
Eating baked potatoes, one after each old story,
Not minding black soot smearing their mouths.

From the low chimney of the mountain hut
Smoke rises, bearing smell of baking potatoes.

Airplane

That propeller at its head
Spins much faster than
The windmill at a miller's.

When afloat high up in the air,
It does not spin so fast as when
The plane soars up from the land.
Maybe it is now short of breath.

The airplane cannot
Wave its wings up and down,
The way birds do.
And always
It yells so loudly.
Maybe now it is out of breath.

Rain in Sunshine

It descends like a shy lady.
Let's all welcome the rain
That falls softly and gently.

Wishing me to grow fast and tall,
As the corn stalks do,
The sun is smiling,
Looking tenderly at me.

Look at the bridge in the sky,
The rainbow with many a color.
Let us sing together joyfully.

Friends, come here to me.
Let us dance together.
The sun is smiling at us,
Happy to see us together.

Broomstick

"We cut like this, like this, it turns into a jacket."
"But cut this way, and it turns into a big gun."
    My sister and I
    Cut paper with scissors,
    Then Mom hit each of us,
    On our butts,
    With her broomstick,
    For we made the floor messy.

    "No, no,
    That nasty broomstick
    Did hit us, sure it did,
    For it hated to sweep the floor."
We put the broomstick in the closet to punish it.
Then, next morning Mom raised a hell,
Looking for that ugly broomstick.

An Old Couple of Roof Tiles

On a rainy evening an old couple of roof tiles,
Maybe because they miss their only son lost,
Stroking each other's curved back,
Drip ceaseless tears, unable to stop weeping.

On the roof of a palace an old couple of roof tiles,
Maybe because they miss their happy olden days,
Caressing each other's wrinkled cheeks,
Cast their eyes upon the lofty sky silently.

Map on a Sleeping Pad

That map drawn on a sleeping pad
    hung spread on a rope to get dried.
That map my younger brother drew
    last night pissing on the pad.

Is it the map of the starry land
    he visited in dream to see Mom?
Is it the map of Manchuria, where
    Pa has gone to make money?

Chicks

"Pyo, pyo, pyo,
Give me milk, Mom,"
The chicks squeaked.

"Cok, cok, cok,
Wait, my babies,"
The hen answered.

A short while later,
All the chicks entered
The warm bosom of the hen,
All of them, all.

My Old Home
—Sung in Manchuria—

Why did I come here,
    Dragging worn straw sandals?
Across the Tuman River,
    To this bleak land?

Beneath the sky yon south,
    My dear homeland in the south,
Where my dear mother lives,
    My dear home in the south—

Clam Shell

The freckled clam shell,
The clam shell that
My sister picked at seashore—

This is a land in the North,
And the clam shell is
A pretty, dear toy to play with—

While playing with it rolling,
I lost one of the two shells,
Making the one left miss its pal—

The freckled clam shell
Also longs, as I do, too,
The sound of the waves, of the sea—

The Hill of Turgenev

I was walking up the hill. . . .
Then three beggar boys passed by me.
The first boy was carrying a basket, slung over his shoulder, filled with empty bottles, tin-cans, metal pieces, worn socks, and what not.
So was the second boy;
So was the third.
Their shaggy hair, sooty faces, bloodshot teary eyes, discolored and pale lips, threadbare patches covering their loins, and bare feet bleeding—
Ah, what dreadful penury has swallowed up these young boys!
Pity welled in me.
So I searched my pockets—
A thick wallet, a watch, a handkerchief. . . I had all I needed.
But I did not have the courage to part with them;
I only kept feeling them in my pockets, wondering what to do.
Having made up my mind to have a friendly talk, I called, "Hello, boys!"
The first boy only turned his bloodshot eyes to me;
So did the second one;
So did the third.
Then, whispering to one another, as I was an intruder, they walked away over the hill.
There was no one on the hill. Only the thickening dusk was billowing toward me.

PROSE

Shooting at the Moon

Now that all the bustle has quieted down and the tick-tock of the clock is clearly audible, night must have deepened quite a bit. Now is the time to push the book I have been reading away from my pillow, and after arranging my sleeping pad, to put on my sleepwear. With the click of turning off the electric bulb, I lie down on my bed close by the window, when I realize that I have not been aware that it is a bright moonlit night outside. Is it another benefit of the bright electric light?

My shabby room soaked in the moonlight does not turn into a beautiful drawing; it looks more like a sad cabin of a ship. The grid of the window shone by the moonlight casts its shadow on my forehead, my nose, my lips, till it reaches the back of my hands folded upon my chest, to tickle my heart. The sound of breathing of the one lying next to me makes the room turn into a dreadful space of confinement. As I look out of the window with eyes widened to suppress childlike bewilderment, the sky in autumn is clear, as it should, and the thick pinewood is like a brush drawing in ink. The moonbeams shower on every pine branch, and make the watcher feel as if he were about to hear the sound of the wind blowing. Now all I can hear are the tick-tock of the clock, the sound of breathing, and the chirp of the crickets. Even this dorm noisy with bustle—hasn't it sunk into quietude deeper than that of a temple?

I am now deeply immersed in thoughts, such as owning a lovely girl for adoration, or lapsing in nostalgic feelings for my childhood hometown; but there are also some indescribable sentiments not to be so easily expressed.

The more I dig into what H has written in his letter to cross the sea, I realize how indescribably subtle the feelings between one man and another are. To him, who is overly sentimental, autumn must have come unavoidably.

Doesn't his letter sound too sentimental? A part of it reads:

"Friend, I am now weeping, while writing. Tonight again, the moon has risen, wind blows, and, as I am a man, I can smell autumn. Tears arising from sentiments, tears brewed in the heart of an aspirant for fine arts, are to be stopped tonight."

At the end his epistle I read the lines:

"It will be a truthful act of yours to banish me once and for all."

I can detect the nuance of what he wrote. But the truth is: I have never said anything that would hurt him, and have never sent him a line that might bruise his feelings. As I peruse on this issue, I cannot help but put all the blame on autumn.

Though it would be presumption for an immature person to make such a conclusion, a friend is, after all, a burden on one's heart, and friendship is, indeed, like water contained in a precarious cup ready to spill. Who will dare deny this? As they say, finding a friend is hard; then, what a pain it is to lose one? It entails the pain of having a portion of one's flesh sliced off.

Once I realize that I am in the garden, I don't have to be boggled by such silly questions as "Did I hop over the window sill?" or "Did I open the door of my room to come out of it?" or "Why did I step out of my room?" The only task left for me is to stand before a cosmos that feels shy at the chirp of a cricket, and, like the shadow of the statue of Dr. Billings, feel sad. That's all. I don't have any inclination to transfer this thought of mine to another person. The clothes I wear are as sensitive as my body, and they feel no less chilly in the moonbeams; and autumn dew gives such chill as tears welling in an immature young man's eyes.

When my body is immobilized while I carry on my steps, autumn is there in the pond, along with deep night, trees, and the moon, as well.

At such a moment, I blame autumn, and feel like blaming the moon. I grab a stone that I managed to hold in my hand, and throw it toward the moon with all my might. What catharsis! The moon is shattered to pieces! But when the sudden wave of surprise subsides, the moon soon regains its former shape. As I look on the sky, the indomitable moon is beaming, as if ridiculing me. . . .

I collect firm and stiff tree boughs to choose one fit for a bow, strong enough, and tie a string onto it to make a bow. Then, using a strong and stiff stalk of reed, as if it were an arrow, I shoot at the moon, with the heart of a warrior.

Where a Shooting Star Fell

It is night. The sky is dark with exceedingly blue tinge almost turning into thick gray, but the stars are twinkling distinctly. Not only this blinding darkness pervades, but the cold air makes one shudder. There is a young man who sneers at himself in the midst of this heavy air. Let us call him "I."

My embryonic being came into existence in this very darkness, and I grew up in it. And it seems that I subsist still in it. Now I am pawing the air, not knowing whereto I should be bound. I look gaunt and pale, indeed, as if I were the one all the agonies of the century had come to focus on. A fleeting impression is that there is neither a firm foundation that supports me nor an oppressive burden that heavily weighs down on me; but the reality is not quite so. I am not free, at all. I am only a spot that floats around in the empty air, as does a dayfly that, though unseen, undeniably exists. If my presence were as flimsy and ephemeral as that of a dayfly, it would be a relief! But the truth is, it is not so.

It seems that, on the symmetrically opposite side, there is another spot—that of brightness. I almost feel that, if I try to grab it quickly, it can come within my grip. But as to my not grabbing it, shouldn't I confess that I am not prepared to do so in my mind—rather than blame myself for being a sluggard? Then, it seems that, for me to invite that special guest, called 'happiness,' into my mind, I will have to set up another pretext for so doing.

The time when night was a dreadful drape of darkness was well in the past of my childhood days. And also the thought that night can be a furnace of delight and pleasure is an indigestible lump for me to swallow. Let it suffice that night remains a target worthy of my challenge.

But if all this thought has to remain only in the realm of abstraction, it is a pity. The thought that scenery of small cottages lying in an array, dozing in darkness, can be a subject of lyric poems belongs to the past generation. Today the scenery only provides the background for the unutterable tragedies of the present life.

Let's suppose: a cock crows loudly, beating its wings, to chase off darkness, inviting the new guest of dawning to brighten the world. But there is no reason to be overjoyed about it. Look, even when the dawn has come, the village will still remain poor, and I'll also remain in misery. Therefore, aren't we all bound to stay in limbo between hope and despair?

Here is a tree. It has been an old acquaintance and friend of mine. But that does not mean that I share any affinity with it because of any common traits in character, the shared environment that has nurtured us, and the way of living. To put it easily to understand, it can be presented as an instance of the queer relationship that miraculously exists between two beings, nurtured in two quite opposite environments, yet sharing mutual love.

At first I looked down on the tree as an unhappy creature not worthy of any attention. When I stood before the tree, I felt sad, and pity for it used to well in my heart. But on second thought, I realize that no other creature can be as happy as a tree. Even the rocks that are the hardest spots on the surface of earth, they say, contain nourishing substance, scanty though it may be. Can a tree not let its roots dig into soil, wherever it happens to be? And will it have any complaint about not being allowed to do so anywhere? When the air gets damp, cool wind blows from the pines. Lest a tree get weary with boredom, birds come to sing for it before flying away. When it gets hungry or thirsty, a streak of rain provides relief. It can have a friendly chat with the innumerable stars at night. But, most of all, it doesn't have to worry about confronting a moment to decide the direction of an act. All it has to do is stay right there where it happened to start its growth, whether by man's hand or by sheer chance. While absorbing inexhaustible nourishment from the soil, it can stay in the blessing of the bright sunrays, watching the sky, toward which it can spread its boughs with no limit. Doesn't all this make its life happy?

Tonight, while I fret in anxiety over not being able to come to terms with my mind-boggling question, what sits in the tree's mind seems to be moving into me, and the pain of realizing that I can't feel proud of my being able to 'act' comes upon me. But a senior friend of mine once told me not to believe what he says, simply because he is a senior. Then, must I turn to the wise tree to ask for the direction I should take?

Which way should I turn to? Which is the east? Which way to the west, south, and north? Alas, yon star flickering and streaming! Maybe that spot where the shooting star will fall must be the spot I must head to. Then, star, you should fall exactly on the spot where you should fall.

Flowers Bloom in the Garden

Forsythia, azalea, violet, lilac, dandelion, brier, balsam, wild rose, sweet brier, peony, lily, iris, tulip, carnation, touch-me-not, crape myrtle, sun plant, dahlia, sunflower, cosmos. . . . The day when cosmos sheds petals is not the last day of the Cosmos. Here the blue sky becomes loftier, the multi-colored autumn leaves dye every single branch of the trees, no less than flowers do in springtime; then, as soon as the chirping of the crickets stops, the season of the dyed leaves fleets away, to be taken over by the night when white snow falls layer on layer to soften the earth; then, in the crock pots charcoal burns red, so that many a tale may be told and many a thing happen around it.

My dear readers, you may not presume that I am now writing in a particular season. No, you may suppose it to be any of the four seasons—spring, summer, autumn, or winter. Indeed, spring cannot last for a whole year. However, if I say that, in this garden, spring blooms along with the youths throughout the four seasons, will it be too much of a grandiose self-advertisement? For a flower garden to be born is not a chance happening; it mandates much effort and endurance. By the way, while choosing and collecting some words to compose this poor piece of wring, I realize that I am not smart enough. The fact is, only after having saved words and thoughts in the cells of my body with sheer physical labor for a whole year, rather than with the help of a smart brain, only then can I produce a few lines. Therefore, writing cannot be a joyful pastime for me. Only after having gone through the suffering in spring breeze, having withered in the ennui of exuberance of green, having wept in the sentiment beneath the autumn sky, and having dozed nearby a firepot, immersed in thoughts, only then I complete a year together with these few lines and with my flower garden.

'Swallowing time'—those who have ever stood with the blackboard behind and those who have ever sat facing it will easily understand the meaning of this phrase and its subtle implication—is no doubt a pleasure. No need to harbor a wish to skip a whole day, though it's up to an individual's whim to do so! Getting freed from class just for an hour, when one is worried over having not completed homework, or when one just feels lazy or drowsy on account of languor, is such a welcome relief! Even if a professor couldn't come to class on account of unexpected physical discomfort, students are not prepared to pay their due concern over his ailment. However, we should not hastily conclude that we are simply thoughtless brats glad to waste our precious time. Here is a garden covered with grass in exuberant green and dotted with red flowers here and there while the students laugh, sitting on it. Who knows? One may be able to explore and attain more profound truths and more ample knowledge while loitering there, more so than while wetting a notebook with ink or struggling with printed words, buried in the piles of books.

I can quietly leave my friends and spend this precious hour all by myself, loitering in the garden. What a blessed hour it is, if I can spend it chatting with flowers and grass! I can face them with a genuine heart, and in exchange for it, they welcome me with sweet smile. Is it because of my being overly sentimental that tears well in my eyes to see them smiling at me? Solitude and quietude are beautiful, indeed. Yet to have friends to share a sentiment with is surely a blessing. Among my friends, who like to get together in the garden, there is Mr. A, who confesses that, on the evening when he is forced to write to his parents to ask them to send him money, he can barely write more than a few lines; Mr. B, who admits that, when the long-awaited document of bank-transaction (what we call "monthly salary") arrives, his hands trembles; Mr. C, who confesses that his love-fever has deprived him of the pleasures of eating and sleeping; Mr. D, who says that, unable to cope with the ideological conflicts going on in his mind, he may end up killing himself, and so forth. I can understand the nature of all their sufferings, as if they were my own, and we all can embrace one another's anguish.

I may have remained more obsessed with such ordinary stuffs as "wind," "clouds," "sunlight," "trees," and "friendship," rather than clinging to such grandiose issues as "weltanschauung" and "outlook on life." Does this statement of mine sound like distortion of a true fact? Or should it be taken as a statement made to blur my truthful image? They say that young people nowadays do not quite measure up to the traditional moral standard. They say the students don't pay enough respect to their teachers. True, indeed. We should feel ashamed. But should we be driven out to the wild field, bearing all the burden of shame and guilty feeling? If a teacher of ours can understand the nature of our pain, is willing to reach out to offer a soothing stroke, then, despite our poor moral attainment, we shall respect him whole-heartedly. Even if I encounter an enemy in the street of good will and warm heart, I shall hold his hand and arm and burst into tears.

Though the world is becoming more and more unsettled year after year with the disturbing roar of the cannons, we still remain in harmony and mutual understanding, while maintaining the old values. Is it a reaction counterbalancing the ongoing flow of the times?

Though spring goes, summer goes, and autumn goes, to make cosmos shed petals, it is not the last day of the universe. There ought to be a season for leaves turning yellow and red. But should we, while treading on frost, only prepare ourselves for the ice that will thicken soon? No, while treading on the leaves covered with frost, we should believe that spring will soon come, though it seems far away. And, in the meantime, many a thing will happen around the firepot that emanates warmth.

The End and the Beginning

A terminal becomes a station where a ride begins. And a station where a ride begins becomes a terminal.

In the morning and in the evening, I repeat the same routine ride. There is a reason for it. In the midst of an exuberant pine wood, which could have been a fine retreat for the renowned monk, the Reverend Sŏsan, stands a house all by itself. Though an isolated one, the house can be proud of its residents. In it swarm good-looking young men, who talk with a variety of intonation and vocabulary, living under the same roof, as if to present a full array of the dialects of the Eight Provinces of the country. There is no legal mandate, but it has become a sanctuary forbidden to ladies. If an iron-hearted woman happens to step into the house, thereby violating its sanctity, the incident would cause much curiosity in all of us, and each room would become the manufacturer of an attention-calling rumor. In this semi-monastic life I have been able to feel sound and safe, as if I were inside a turbo shell.

An incident that leads to a grave consequence always has its origin, not in any noteworthy event, but in a haphazard happening that does not call much of our attention.

It was a snowy day. A friend of my roommate's dropped by to kill time for an hour or so before catching the train that would take him to the town, and I happened to overhear their conversation.

"Hey, are you planning to become a ghost stuck to this house?"

"Isn't it a nice place where I can concentrate on my studies?"

"Do you think that turning the leaves of a book over is enough? What you can see outside while riding a tramcar, what you happen to witness at a station, and whatever incident you encounter inside a train, all of these is part of life. Getting immersed in the atmosphere caused by struggle for life, thinking about it, and analyzing the cause and effect of all this turmoil— Yes, will it not be really 'educational,' in the true sense of the word? Hey, pal, turning the leaves of a book, talking flippantly about life in general and society in particular, should be pushed far back to the Sixteenth Century. Once and for all, relent, and make up your mind to come out to town!"

Though it was not for me, I leaned my ears to his admonition, which sounded quite convincing to me. Searching for truth in life, while not only being stuck to this house but staying away from general humanity, cannot but be an act of pleasure-seeking; an act of pleasure-seeking cannot be a serious part of real life; and, if not related to real life, study is useless. So, having concluded that study should be grounded on real life, I decided to enter the town within the next few days. After that decision was made, I have been repeating my daily routine of entering the town.

I thought I would be the only one to feel the fresh touch of the morning air in the town; but the pavements were already busy with the bustle of the footsteps, and whenever the tramcar stopped, it allowed so many people to squeeze into it, not caring about where it would unload them. And none of the old people, young people, children, indeed none of them, had hands free from things to carry. These bundles of wrapped up load must be their shabby packs of life—their packs of ennui in life, as well.

Let me now scrutinize the face of each one carrying a bundle or two. We may as well skip the faces of the old people, for they have already gone through their long sojourn in life. But the faces of the young ones! Ten out of ten faces of theirs are shadowed with gloom. Hundred out of a hundred faces of theirs bear the trace of misery. Seeing any of them smiling is well beyond the possibility of seeing beans sprouting during the season of drought. The last alternative left is to turn my eyes to children, whose faces ought to be lovely and delightful to watch. But, alas, their faces are too pale! Perhaps they are worried about their teachers' impending scolding about unfinished homework? In any case, their crestfallen faces don't show any tinge of liveliness. My own face must be bearing exactly the same gloom. What a relief that I am unable to see my own face shadowed in dejection! If I had been subjected to the ordeal of confronting my own face as often as I watch other people's faces, I would have been gone long ago!

But let me distrust my eyes and give it up! Watching the sky that stretches over the castle wall is more pleasant. My eyes keep running along the line dividing the sky and the castle wall, which has been restored over the ruins of the wall built for defense of the royal town. Those of us who have been living outside of the wall cannot even guess what has happened and is happening inside. The only expectation left for us is to reach where the castle wall ends.

But we'd better not harbor too much expectation. Where the castle wall stops running, there begins a row of buildings for public or commercial missions, such as the Governor's Office Building, the Administration Hall for the Province, the Reference Library of some sort, the Postal Service Building, some newspaper company building, the fire station, a stock company building, some ministry's building, a tailor's shop, an antic item dealer's shop, and so forth. Suddenly a sign board advertising ice-cream comes into view. I close my eyes, and imagine what a fine caricature it would turn out to be, if I take a shot of the sign board advertising ice cream in the middle of the snowy winter, occupying a space well beyond what it deserves. Indeed, how many people these days are not in a similar situation wherein that ice-cream advertising sign board is? That ice-cream advertisement sign board must be missing sultry summer.

As I immerse in thoughts with my eyes closed, there is one thing that bothers me. It is what they call 'moral code of behavior,' which mandates forced obedience. Feeling that someone may be scowling at me in his or her thought, disgusted with the spectacle of a young man brazen-facedly occupying a seat with his eyes closed not to see anyone who deserves it, I open my eyes. I feel relieved to realize that nobody up till now may have felt disgusted at my brazen-faced behavior, not that I don't have to offer my seat to anyone for the moment.

A friend of mine, who is quick in making conclusions, once said: "Someone you meet in a tramcar is an enemy, and someone you meet in a train is a friend." I agreed with him, thinking that what he said contained a certain degree of truth. While being forced to rub against someone in a crowded tramcar, one may as well utter a kind greeting, saying "What a fine day!" or "Where will you get off?" But all these sullen faces, not to mention the stubborn silence, make all the passengers look like irreconcilable enemies! If there happens to be a person, who is willing to extend that much kindness to those sitting or standing nearby, he or she will be looked upon either as a lunatic or an idiot! Not so in a train cabin. People exchange their name cards, talk about their hometowns, whereto they are going, without feeling any discomfort. They even show their concern about the hardship of others' journey, as if it were their own. What a tender and heart-warming way of living life!

While I remain absorbed in contemplation, I pass by the South Gate. Suppose someone happens to say to me: "You pass by the South Gate twice a day. Do you watch it every time?" If he throws such an apparently silly question to measure my intellectual level, I'll have to get stunned. As I try to recall, since I started riding the tramcar to get into the town, I don't seem to have paid any attention to the South Gate, not even once, not to mention "every time." Well, since it has nothing to do with my personal life, it is natural. However, here is a piece of lesson. When anything occurs too often, it becomes an ordinary matter.

Though it may be an irrelevant episode, let me tell you about it, so that we can somewhat relieve us of boredom.

There was a gentleman, one who did very well deserve that appellation in his own right in his hometown. After making his first trip to Seoul, he returned home, and, using the Seoul people's intonation and words he had managed to pick up during his brief sojourn in that town, he arduously described the scenery of the streets of Seoul, using both his hands and tongue: how the magnificent South Gate, shining with the grandeur of the time past, confronted him with welcoming note, when he got out of the train station; how big was the Governor's Office Building was; what a variety of animals and birds were being kept in the zoo in the Chang-gyŏng Palace Garden; how the Dŏksu Palace made him feel nostalgic for the glory of the bygone dynasty; how dizzy he felt when he was confined in an elevator of Hwa-shin Department Store building; how bright the Myŏngdong Street at night was like daytime; what a big crowd of people billowed and ebbed in the streets; how ferociously that monster machines called 'tramcars' were rushing, yelling and squeaking, like metallic monsters, and so forth. He was bragging about his experience, as if that capital town had been built just for his own sake. Well, all this is understandable. But a mischievous and malicious listener asked him:

"The calligraphy on the panel of the South Gate is magnificent, isn't it?"

Well, the answer to this question was no less unprepared:

"A virtuoso's brush-wielding, indeed! Each of the three characters—'Nam' and 'Dae' and 'Mun'—looked as if it were alive, wriggling and stretching!"

It was an answer worthy of a man who wanted to brag about his worthy experience of exploring the former royal town. I wonder, though, how he would have been thrown into bewilderment, had he been asked what was there near the top of Ahyŏn Hill, or, to choose a place not so much removed from the center of the town, what's in the back alley of Chong-no Avenue.

I make my journey's terminus turn into its starting point, for the place where I get off is my journey's terminus, and the place where I get on board is its starting point. During that brief moment I let myself be swept into a crowd, when I become a being of nonentity. There is no way for me to exert my humanity to this crowd, for there is no way for me to measure all the joy, grief, or pain each of them feels. It is too indiscernible. Maybe we become superficial too easily when frequency and quantity increase. Maybe because each one becomes busy to take care of oneself at such time.

Treading on the signal, the train departs, swishing. Knowing that it will not take me home, I feel my heart throbbing for some unknown reason. Our train crawls on, stopping at temporary stations, whenever it gets short of breath. Everyday I see a bunch of women standing in a row on the platform, each one holding a bundle or something, the purpose of which one may vaguely guess at. All of them are of nubile age, but, judging from the way they are dressed, they don't look like those who are headed to factories. They are standing there like modest ladies waiting for a train—or, for evaluative judgment. However, it is not recommended to evaluate the beauty of a woman hastily through the glass window. The law of superficiality may be applicable to this case, too. Apparently transparent, glass is not to be trusted for accurate observation.

Sometimes it can squeeze and distort a face, narrow down its forehead, transform a nose to that of a horse, make a chin look like a clam shell, and perform other mischievous deeds without feeling any remorse or guilty feelings. For those who are in the position to make a judgment, these trickeries of glass will not incur any loss. But what about those whose beauty has to be evaluated? For the latter, (who knows?) the luck that was about to come may run away. In any case, no matter how transparent a cover may be, it is proper and justifiable to peel if off cleanly.

At long last a tunnel is waiting with its mouth wide open. How sad it is that in the middle of a city route a tunnel, not a subterranean railway, is waiting? This monster called 'tunnel' is the Dark Age in human history, and the emblem of the agony of the journey of life. For no special reason, the wheels rumble so loudly. Nauseatingly obnoxious smoke steals into the cabin. However, the world of brightness will come soon.

When the train comes out of the tunnel, I see the workers busy with the double-rail construction going on these days. I saw them working when I took the first train. They are still working at this late hour, when I am on my way back home. I cannot figure out when they start working and when they stop working for the day. These are the apostles of construction work. They don't spare sweat and blood.

While pushing their heavy truck, they let their imagination fly to a faraway place. Having written on a panel of the truck in clumsy calligraphy words like "To Shinkyŏng," "To Peking," or "To Nanjing," they push it, rather than ride on it. Here one can peep into their hearts. Who can adamantly say that this imaginative diversion does not provide some consolation for them going through hard labor?

Now it is about time for me to reverse the order of the beginning and the end. But on the vehicle I ride on, I wish to attach the signboards, "To Shinkyŏng," "To Peking," and "To Nanjing." No, I feel like writing thereon "All around the World." No, if I had a truthful home of mine, I will carry the signboard, "To my Home." If there is a Station of the Age where I'll arrive next, it will be even better.

Index of Titles

Afternoon in a Glen, An 68
Ailing Rose, An 58
Airplane 131
Another Home 43
Apple 122
At a Hospital 32
Autumn Night, An 82
Beloved Memory, A 48
Bidding Farewell 99
Both 116
Boy, A 29
Broomstick 133
Chest (1) 89
Chest (2) 90
Chicks 136
Chickens (1) 85
Chickens (2) 120
Chimney 130
Clam Shell 138
Confession, A 52
Consolation 55
Cosmos 61
Counting the Stars at Night 45
Cricket and I, The 108
Cross, The 39
Dawn Comes with the Baby's Crying 109
Daydreaming 102
Dog, A 126
Downpour 73
Dream Has Shattered 93
Dying Man's Wish, A 66
Echo 107
Eightfold Blessing 56
End and the Beginning, The 150

Firefly Light   115
Firmament   101
Flowers Bloom in the Garden   147
Flowing Street, A   49
Forest   86
Grandpa   114
Hill of Turgenev, The   139
Landscape   76
Lark   96
Letter, A   125
Life and Death   105
Like the Moon   59
Liver   53
Mandol   113
Map on a Sleeping Pad   135
Market   78
Meal Ticket   98
Moonlit Night   77
Morning   81
Mountain Top   88
Mountain Water   57
My Old Home   137
New Road, A   33
Night   79
Old Couple of Roof Tiles, An   134
On Such a Day   94
On the Street   103
Pathos   72
Pattern for Footwear   124
Pensive Moment   71
Pepper Patch, The   60
Pigeons   100
Piro Peak   69
Pockets   118
Poem Written Easily, A   50
Portrait of My Younger Brother, A   62

Primeval Morn (1)   35
Primeval Morn (2)   36
Prologue   27
Rain in Sunshine   132
Rainy Night, A   65
Returning at Night   31
Road, The   44
Road in the Valley, A   84
Sad People, A   41
Sea, The   70
Self-Portrait   28
Shooting at the Moon   143
Sleepless Nights   54
Snow (1)   121
Snow (2)   123
Snowy Map, A   30
Soccer Field in the Afternoon   95
Southern Sky   92
Sparrows   127
Spring (1)   51
Spring (2)   128
Street without Signboards, A   34
Sunflower's Face   110
Sunlight and Wind   111
Sunlit Side, The   87
Temple of Love, The   64
Terrible Hour, A   38
That Single Candle   106
That Woman   74
There's No Such a Thing as Tomorrow   104
Thermometer   75
Till Dawn Breaks   37
Trees   112
Twilight   91
Twilight Turns into a Sea   80
Upon Moran Peak   97

Walk with Your Eyes Closed   42
Washed Clothes Hung over a String   83
What a Lie!   117
What Do They Eat to Live?   129
Where a Shooting Star Fell   145
White Shadows   47
Wind Blows   40
Window   67
Winter   119
Wonder, A   63

About the Translators

Insoo Lee (1916–1950), a pioneer of English studies in Korea, studied at University College, London, earning the degree of B. A. Honors in 1940. Upon completing his studies in England he returned to Korea, and taught at Korea University till 1950, the year of his demise in the aftermath of the Korean War. A compilation of his writings in English, *Inside Cloud Cuckoo Land: the Voice of Korea*, was published by The Association for Textual Study and Production at Troy, Alabama, in 2008.

Sung-Il Lee, born in 1943, studied English literature, earning his Ph. D. at Texas Tech University in 1980. He taught English poetry and drama at Yonsei University from 1981 till he retired in 2009. He is now Professor Emeritus of Yonsei University. He has published ten volumes of Korean poetry in his English translation: *The Wind and the Waves: Four Modern Korean Poets* (1989), *The Moonlit Pond: Korean Classical Poems in Chinese* (1998), *The Brush and the Sword: Kasa, Korean Classical Poems in Prose* (2009), *Blue Stallion: Poems of Yu Chi-whan* (2011), *The Crane in the Clouds: Shijo, Korean Classical Poems in the Vernacular* (2013), *The Vertex: Poems of Yi Yook-sa* (2014), *Nostalgia: Poems of Chung Ji-yong* (2017), *Shedding of the Petals: Poems of Cho Jihoon* (2019), *Do You Know That Faraway Land? Poems of Shin Sŏk-jŏng* (2020), and *Does Spring Come Also to These Ravished Fields? Poems of Yi Sang-hwa* (2022). He received the Grand Prize in translation in The Republic of Korea Literary Awards (1990) and The Korean Literature Translation Award (1999), both given by The Korean Culture and Arts Foundation.

www.ingramcontent.com/pod-product-compliance
Lightning Source LLC
Chambersburg PA
CBHW070453100426
42743CB00010B/1603